WISDOM
of
PUPPIES

© 2008 by Moseley Road Inc.

This 2008 edition published by Metro Books,
by arrangement with Moseley Road Inc.

Art Director: Brian MacMullen
Designer: Eunho Lee
Editor: Ward Calhoun
Photo Researcher: Benjamin DeWalt

Metro Books
122 Fifth Avenue
New York, NY 10011

ISBN: 978-1-4351-0534-8

Printed and bound in China

3 5 7 9 10 8 6 4 2

WISDOM
of
PUPPIES

Compiled by
Ward Calhoun

METRO BOOKS
NEW YORK

"Let age, **not envy**, draw wrinkles on thy cheeks."

–Thomas Browne

"Stuff your **eyes with wonder**, live as if you'd drop dead in ten seconds. **See the world**. It's more fantastic than any dream made or paid for in factories."

–Ray Bradbury

"Memories, **imagination**, old sentiments, and associations are more readily reached through the **sense of smell** than through any other channel."

–*Oliver Wendell Holmes*

"The way to become **rich** is to put all **your eggs** in one basket and then watch that basket."

–Andrew Carnegie

"Family is not an important thing, it's everything."

–Michael J. Fox

"Patience is sorrow's **salve**."

–Charles Churchill

"The **greatest gifts** you can give your children are the roots of **responsibility** and the wings of **independence**."

–Denis Waitley

"The grass **isn't** always greener on the other side!"

–Ricky Gervais

"One of the best ways to **persuade** others is with your ears—by **listening to them**."

–*Dean Rusk*

"Cherish forever
what makes you
unique, 'cuz you're
really a yawn
if it goes."

–Bette Midler

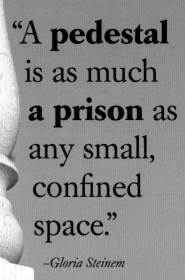

"A **pedestal** is as much **a prison** as any small, confined space."

–*Gloria Steinem*

"**Hide nothing**, for time, which sees all and hears all, exposes all."

–Sophocles

"Gather ye rosebuds
while ye may,
Old Time is still a-flying:
And this same flower
that **smiles today**,
To-morrow will be dying."

–Robert Herrick

"It **isn't** the mountains ahead to climb that **wear you out**; it's the pebble in your shoe."

–*Muhammad Ali*

"I'm just like **everyone**.

I like to feel togetherness with **someone.**

–*Lucinda Williams*

"Let **your tongue speak** what your **heart** thinks."

–Davy Crockett

"Never **lend your car**
to anyone to whom you
have **given** birth."

–Erma Bombeck

"It is good to realize that if **love and peace** can prevail on earth, and if we **can teach our children** to honor nature's gifts, the joys and beauties of the outdoors will be here forever."

–*Jimmy Carter*

"Autumn is a **second spring** when every **leaf** is a flower."

–Albert Camus

"Affection can **withstand** very **severe storms** of vigor, but not a long polar frost of indifference."

–*Sir Walter Scott*

"You don't live in a world all alone.

Your brothers are here too."

–Dr. Albert Schweitzer

"The **Saints** are the Sinners who **keep on** trying."

–Robert Louis Stevenson

"There are no passengers on **spaceship** earth. We are all crew."

–Marshall McLuhan

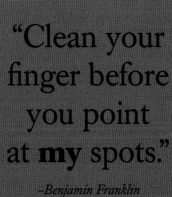

"Clean your
finger before
you point
at **my** spots."

–*Benjamin Franklin*

"The **cure for boredom** is curiosity. There is **no** cure for curiosity."

–Dorothy Parker

"Man is never **watchful** enough **against dangers** that threaten him every hour."

–*Horace*

"**Sharing** is sometimes more demanding than **giving**."

–*Mary Catherine Bateson*

"As a well spent day brings happy **sleep**, so life well used brings happy **death**."

–Leonardo DaVinci

"There are no great things, only small things with **great love**. Happy are those."

–*Mother Teresa*

"Life is either a **daring adventure**

or it is nothing."   –Helen Keller

"Have **compassion for all beings**, rich and poor alike; each has their suffering. Some suffer too much, others too little."

–Buddha

"A face is like the outside of a house, and **most faces**, like most houses, give us an idea of what **we can expect** to find inside."

–Loretta Young

"Heaven is **by favor**;
if it were by merit your dog
would **go in** and
you would stay out."

–*Mark Twain*

"Look **before you leap**
for as you sow,
ye are like to reap."

–Samuel Butler

"Why not **seize the pleasure** at once, how often is happiness destroyed by preparation, foolish preparations."

–*Jane Austen*

"The best place to find **God** is in a garden. You can **dig** for him there."

–George Bernard Shaw

"Re-examine all you
have been told . . .
dismiss that which
insults your soul."

–*Walt Whitman*

"**Every moment** is a golden one for him

who has **the vision** to recognize it as such."

—Henry Miller

"Nothing makes one **feel so strong** as a call for help."

–Pope Paul VI

"One should either be **sad or joyful**. Contentment is a warm sty for eaters and sleepers."

–Eugene O'Neill

"Do not bite at the bait of pleasure, till you know there is no hook beneath it."

–Thomas Jefferson

"**Intensity** is so **much more** becoming in the young."

–Joanne Woodward

"The best way to find out if you can **trust somebody** is to trust them."

–*Ernest Hemingway*

"We may have all come on different ships, but we're **in the same boat** now."

–*Martin Luther King, Jr.*

"Growth **itself** contains the germ of happiness."

–*Pearl S. Buck*

"Dogs are **wise**. They crawl away into a quiet corner and **lick their wounds** and do not rejoin the world until they are whole once more."

–*Agatha Christie*

"Good taste is better than bad taste, but **bad taste is better** than no taste."

–*Arnold Bennett*

"I would rather have a big burden and **a strong back**, than a weak back and a caddy to carry life's luggage."

–*Elbert Hubbard*

"When you're thirsty and it seems that you could drink the entire ocean—that's **faith**; when you start to drink and finish only a glass or two—that's **science**."

–*Anton Chekhov*

"**Mystery** creates **wonder** and wonder is the basis of man's **desire** to understand."

–Neil Armstrong

"If you want to make your **dreams** come true, the first thing you have to do is **wake up.**"

–J.M. Power

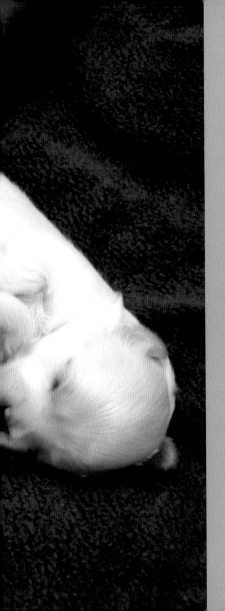

"Father asked us what was God's **noblest work**. Anna said men, but I said babies. Men are often bad; **babies** never are."

–*Louisa May Alcott*

"If a man does not **keep pace** with his companions, perhaps it is because he **hears a different drummer**. Let him step to the music which he hears, however measured or far away."

–Henry David Thoreau

"The hardest job
kids face today is learning
good manners
without seeing any."

–*Fred Astaire*

"Silence is a true friend who never betrays."

—Confucius

"Jump into the middle of things, get your hands **dirty**, fall flat on your face, and then reach for the stars."

–Ben Stein

"Don't look back.
Something might be
gaining on you."

–Satchel Paige

PICTURE CREDITS